Hubble Stitch

Instructions & Inspiration for this
Adaptable New Lace Beadwork Technique

Melanie de Miguel

 INTERWEAVE™

www.interweave.com

Originally published as Let's Hubble: A Journey into the Brand New Beadwork Stitch by Melanie de Miguel, SRA Books, UK.

19 18 17 16 15   5 4 3 2 1

Distributed in Canada by Fraser Direct
100 Armstrong Avenue
Georgetown, ON, Canada L7G 5S4
Tel: (905) 877-4411

a content + ecommerce company

Distributed in the U.K. and Europe by F&W MEDIA INTERNATIONAL
Brunel House, Newton Abbot, Devon, TQ12 4PU, England
Tel: (+44) 1626 323200, Fax: (+44) 1626 323319
E-mail: enquiries@fwmedia.com

Distributed in Australia by Capricorn Link
P.O. Box 704, S. Windsor NSW, 2756 Australia
Tel: (02) 4560 1600, Fax: (02) 4577 5288
E-mail: books@capricornlink.com.au

SRN: 16BD06
ISBN-13: 978-1-63250-500-2

EDITED BY Sue Richardson and Kerry Bogert
DESIGNED BY Courtney Kyle
PHOTOGRAPHY BY Michael Wicks

CONTENTS

INTRODUCTION

A New Beadwork Stitch

A New Beadwork Stitch

It all started with a very perky picot...

I once designed a bracelet, which I called Lorenzo, having been inspired by the treasures of the fabulous Medici dynasty while on a holiday in Florence. One of the main components was a herringbone stitched "wing" connector that was tipped with pretty little picots. I constructed each of those picots in the usual way, by picking up three beads for the stitch – I had always seen them made in this way and simply accepted that method. When I had progressed somewhat with the bracelet I suddenly noticed, much to my disappointment, that the picots had effectively drooped and were no longer little triangles, but more like a line of three beads. No amount of picking or prodding at them with a needle could revitalize them permanently, so I wondered if there was a way to prevent this from happening in the first place. To stop the central tip bead of the picot from dropping down between the two outer ones, something had to hold them all together. Then came the serendipity moment; it was so simple – when you work a normal herringbone stitch and place a picot bead in the subsequent row, that picot bead will sit nice and perky forever more. It's the thread between the two beads of the herringbone stitch that provides a perch for the picot bead, preventing it from sinking down. So, in order to work this lovely, perky little picot into the design, I knew I had to make two passes for each picot – the first pass sets the two base beads in place, and the picot tip bead is positioned on the second pass. I've now incorporated this "super picot" into many of my designs.

So what exactly is Hubble stitch? It can best be described as a blend of herringbone and ladder stitch and a close cousin of right angle weave (RAW), all rolled into one. Each stitch is constructed in two phases, or passes, based on my super picot, which means beads are picked up and a circle is made on the first pass, with the tip bead picked up and set in place on the second pass.

The circular thread paths made in Hubble stitches are similar to those in RAW, but the big difference is that each stitch within a row is individual, that is, it's not linked to its neighbor by a bead, allowing lots of movement and slinkiness to the textile formed. This separation and individuality of each stitch also confers a beautiful, lacy quality to the beadwork.

Why the funny name? There were a few reasons. For a start, when I write instructions, I often abbreviate stitch names, so herringbone becomes HB and ladder stitch becomes L; throw them together and you get HBL, which is Hubble when read phonetically. The name also instantly appealed to me, as I am a great admirer of the Hubble space telescope, and its vital role in cosmology. So, while my explorations with Hubble stitch have been on a much tinier scale, I am hugely inspired by the wonderful potential of this stitch and all its applications, and most of all I am very excited to be sharing it with you.

Chapter by chapter, I have set out to guide you in a logical progression, through the discovery of the different forms of Hubble, graduating from the most basic stitch to more complex and interesting forms and combinations. Each stage is illustrated by one or more projects with further variation ideas and suggestions,

all designed to help you practice Hubbling and become really at home with it. You will also find workshop tips scattered throughout the book; the idea of these tips is to zero in on any particular issue and troubleshoot, or just make things a bit easier, as if I am there with you in a workshop.

I have now been working on and developing Hubble stitch for two years and never cease to be amazed and delighted by the simple beauty of basic and 2-Drop Hubble, and, in particular, how the outline definition of the stitch changes according to the color and finish of the chosen beads.

In this book you will encounter basic Hubble, 2-Drop, 3-Drop, Spaced Out Hubble (both Horizontal and Vertical), Hubble-in-the-round (Circular and Tubular Hubble), and Inverted Hubble! However, while writing I have continued to explore and develop lots of

interesting ways of mani- pulating Hubble stitch, and you will meet these in book two.

As this is a brand-new stitch, I would ask you to set aside concepts and understandings of existing stitch pathways, such as RAW, herringbone- and ladder stitch. To many beaders these will be "dear old friends" that can be conjured up automatically, but when you first begin to play with Hubble stitch you may find the thread path is alien to you, particularly when making the foundation row. The key is to keep an open mind and have some real fun with it.

You don't have to be an experienced beader to master Hubbling; with just a little practice you will find Hubble stitch flows beautifully, and I'm certain that once you have played with the basic stitch, you will be champing at the bit to try out all the possibilities.

CHAPTER
ONE

*Materials, Tools,
and Terms*

Materials and Tools

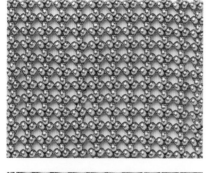

Basic and 2-Drop Hubble stitches have distinctive shapes and are very beautiful when clearly defined. Using metallic, matte, and frosted beads can really help to emphasize the Hubble shapes in the textile, whereas transparent, subtle colors don't seem to make as strong a statement unless they have a pretty AB finish.

No beading book seems to be complete without the materials and tools section, but if you're anything like me, you can't wait to skip over those pages and get to the meaty bits – the techniques and designs! So I made a conscious decision not to include long lists and descriptions of beading materials and tools in this book, because you don't need anything unusual in order to Hubble. However, for both new beadworkers and experienced alike, there are materials suggestions for each project so you won't be thrown in at the deep end!

Having said that, to help you prepare for the projects in this book I would like to make a few suggestions regarding beading thread, needles, pliers, and choice of bead color and finish to optimize your Hubbling experience.

When it comes to beading thread, you must feel comfortable and confident with it, and there are a number of choices available. I am an avid fan of Fireline, particularly 4lb test, as it's an excellent all-round thread for working with seed beads ranging in size from as large as 6° to as small as Czech 15° (which is equivalent to the Japanese size 18°). It is strong and pre-waxed, which gives it a fabulous "sliding" quality, allowing you to snuggle up the beads without any stretching occurring, and therefore helping you to maintain an even tension in your beadwork.

All the projects in this book can be worked using size 12 needles, but when size 15° Czech Charlotte seed beads are used in the project you will need to switch to smaller, size 14 needles, for example, when attaching and fixing the daisy spacers to the clasp loops.

For ease of threading the Fireline through fine needle eyes, I always flatten the end 1" (2cm) of the thread with flat nose pliers (just a few gentle squishes do the trick), so it's very helpful to have a pair handy. Along with the flat nose pliers, I generally keep a pair each of round nose pliers and wire cutters close by, and you will need these for some of the projects.

Choose seed beads that are of good quality and consistent in size and shape, as this will help you produce beautiful Hubble textiles that are satisfyingly smooth and even. Also be aware that mixing different makes of seed bead within a project may produce disappointing results, as different manufacturers produce beads of slightly different dimensions, even though they are labelled with the same size number.

Although I have avoided working Hubble stitch in cylinder beads, e.g., Miyuki Delicas, as their strong, flat, cylindrical lines don't complement the stitch shape as elegantly as the soft round edges of seed beads, I have experimented with them and they Hubble together in an interesting way because of their large holes, so they shouldn't be ignored altogether. To a much lesser extent, this is also true of silver-lined seed beads, because they too tend to have a rather cylindrical shape, although some of them are so delicious that they've just got to be used! So, let this be a rough guide to choices of bead color and finish; try some of the suggested colorways in the projects and then experiment for yourself.

Notes and Terms

To work any of the instructions and projects in this book, it's helpful to familiarize yourself with the terms I use:

Wingspan	The length of thread to be used. Holding the end of the thread in one hand and the reel in the other just spread your arms wide apart like wings and cut that length.
Snuggle up	This is my way of describing the action of sliding beads or stitches up close to each other to make them touch, leaving very little, if any, thread visible between them. For Hubble, the stitches **only just need to touch**. This is of particular importance in the foundation row.
Tail thread	If it isn't specified at the start of a project or element, always leave a tail thread of approximately 6" (15cm). This is an optimum length both for gripping your beadwork and for ease of sewing in at the end.
Finish off	Means weave back through your work, making a few half hitch knots along the way, and cut the thread where it emerges.
Work in	Means join in a new thread thus: Insert the needle into the beadwork a short distance away from the point where you wish to begin beading again; weave through to where you want to emerge, following the previous thread paths, and making a few half hitch knots on the way, then cut off the tail end of the new thread.
Tension	It is very important that you always maintain an even tension while working in Hubble. It really shouldn't be tight, just smooth and consistent, which will help you produce lovely, slinky Hubble textiles. The exception is when you are Hubbling around an object, for example, a bead or cabochon. In this instance you may need to increase the tension to ensure a good, tight fit, with no visible threads.
Cast on	This term refers to making the foundation stitches, so "cast on ten Hubble stitches" means you should work a foundation row of ten Hubble stitches.

CHAPTER TWO

Hubble Stitch

Hubble Stitch

When teaching I often try to draw parallels in beadwork with recognizable, common shapes to help students position their needles in the correct spot. For example, peyote stitch is characterized by a one-up, one-down bead formation, which I think looks like the turrets on a medieval castle, so I call the uppermost beads "turret beads". I've had a lot of fun going through this mental process while Hubbling, and you'll soon see why.

As a general rule, when you start a piece of beadwork, no matter how experienced you are, the initial stitches tend to be fiddly, and often the foundation row of the chosen stitch is worked differently. It's only on the second row that things settle down and the true stitch can be worked. The news is that Hubble stitch is no exception!

We'll start with the basic Hubble stitch, and along the way you will begin to encounter the terminology. I will go into a lot of detail in these early stages because I want you to have fun, not trouble with Hubble!

When I first began discovering all the Hubbling possibilities, I made little test swatches of around six stitches by six rows, using about 40" (1m) thread and one color of size 11° seed beads. I would suggest this is a good way to start getting to know Hubble, then try out the projects at the end of each chapter.

Foundation Row:

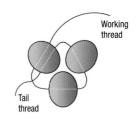

Phase 1: Pick up 3 beads and make a ring by passing the needle again through the first bead picked up, in the same direction.

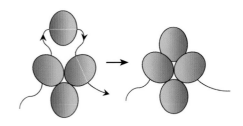

Phase 2: Pick up 1 bead. Pass the needle through the adjacent bead of the ring, settling the new bead firmly in place.

That completes one foundation Hubble stitch.

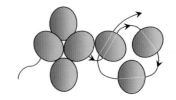

Repeat **Phase 1**. Do not be tempted to try and pass the needle into any beads of the previous stitch.

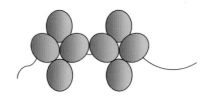

Repeat **Phase 2** to complete a 2nd foundation Hubble. Now snuggle up!

Within a row, the beads of individual adjacent Hubble stitches should be touching, but not so tightly that they are actually under one another, as this will corrupt the straight line formation. If you find that you have snuggled up a stitch too tightly to its next door neighbor, just grip the beadwork and slip the tip of your nail gently between the two stitches to ease them apart slightly, so they only just touch.

This all takes a little practice but it will become automatic as you progress.

5 Work some more Hubbles, snuggling up along the way.

Heads up! Take a close look at your little line of stitches; notice that each foundation Hubble stitch has a definite shape, with a bottom, which is the 3-bead base of Phase 1, and a top, which is the picot tip bead of Phase 2.

Workshop Tip 1: *In reality, as you can see in the image above, the stitches aren't actually lying exactly as depicted in the step 5 diagram; some are pointing upwards and some downwards, because they are each simply connected by a single thread. However, they can be individually swivelled around to the upright position* **as you work the 2nd row,** *so don't try to correct them before continuing; it is not a problem at all and, in fact, is an exciting characteristic of Hubble that allows lots of possibilities for variation.*

Workshop Tip 2: *Look very closely at the junction between each of the Hubbles in the image above. Where there are two adjacent Hubbles in the upright position, note how neatly they are just touching. Now look at a junction between a Hubble that is upright and one that is upside down (and there are a few) – there's a tiny gap! What has happened here is that as I stitched them, I made sure they just touched and they were upright together; however, once I let them go to move on to the next stitch, one of them has swivelled round and the gap appeared. This doesn't mean I have to go back and tighten them up, as they were perfect beforehand. To tighten them would cause definite curving and ruin the desired straight line. When the 2nd row is worked and they are upright once more, the gap will disappear.*

To me, when the stitches are upright, they look just like a little row of table foosball players, with their downward-pointing bodies, and their arms and heads held high – little Henrys, joyfully shouting "Hooray."

When they're upside down, they could be doing headstands!

So, to help you understand which beads I refer to in the instructions, the Phase 2 bead is the head bead, the bead vertically opposite pointing downwards and central is the body bead, and the remaining two beads on either side of the head are the arm beads; the body and arm beads constitute the bead base.

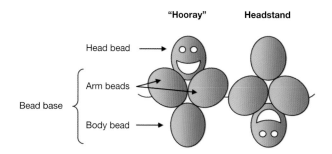

While there are three beads in the foundation bead base of basic Hubble, the number will change when we progress to 2-Drop Hubble and again for 3-Drop Hubble, but we'll deal with those stitches in the next chapter. Lastly, another way of recognizing whether your Hubbles are upright or not, is that **the thread between stitches always emerges from under their arms**.

It is really important you recognize which way is up for the foundation stitches because it has implications in subsequent rows, and a single Henry doing a headstand will really show up against the others and spoil the uniformity.

Now it's time to step up and work the second row, bearing in mind that the head beads of your foundation row Hubbles will become the body beads of the new row. You'll see!

6 To step up, pass around the Hubble to emerge from the head bead.

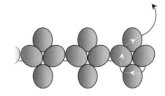

Workshop Tip 3: *Note that when you have stepped up, the thread is always emerging away from the beadwork, ready for each new row.*

2nd Row:

7 **1st Stitch – Phase 1**: Pick up 2 beads and make a ring by passing through the head bead below (from which the thread was emerging) in the same direction; continue on through the first bead of the 2 just picked up.

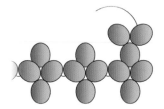

Heads up! This has effectively replicated the ring of 3 beads that you made for each foundation stitch Phase 1, and positioned you ready to place the head bead for Phase 2.

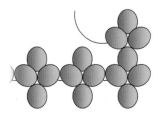

8 **Phase 2**: Pick up 1 bead and pass down through the adjacent arm bead.

Heads up – and this is a BIG heads up! Look carefully at the next foundation Hubble and ask yourself this very, very important question:

"Is he a happy, Hooray Henry Hubble, or is he standing on his head?"

You will have to ask that same question for every new stitch of the entire second row. Once the second row is complete it will no longer matter, as the Hubbles will be set in their positions and they won't be able to swivel anymore.

Let's move on...

9 **2nd Stitch – Phase 1:** Pick up 2 beads. **Ask the question** to ensure the next Hubble is saying Hooray (if it's not, then swivel it around like a foosball player – you can do this with the tip of the needle in the head bead), and pass through the head bead in the direction of the previous stitch in this row, in other words, **backstitch**!

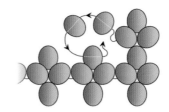

10 (Still in **Phase 1**): Continue on through the first of the 2 beads just picked up, in the same direction as before, ready to place the new head bead.

Snuggle up!

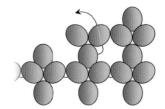

11 **Phase 2**: Pick up 1 bead and pass through the adjacent arm bead (the same as for a foundation Hubble stitch).

Complete the 2nd row, working the Hubbles as for the 2nd stitch. Step up exactly as you did at the end of the foundation row, and remember, for the 3rd and subsequent rows you don't need to ask the question any more, because they'll all be shouting **HOORAY!**

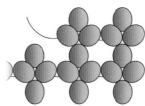

SPECTRUM

Hubble stitch has spatial direction and order, and the color changes in this simple, fun bracelet show it off to the max! The daisy spacers are a delightful feature and an excellent way of hiding the loops of the clasp, rendering it unobtrusive. The Hubble strip is worked horizontally which means it grows widthways not lengthways; this necessitates a long foundation row, providing an excellent opportunity for you to practice both casting on and "asking the question" throughout the long second row.

The seven colors of the spectrum – Violet, Indigo, Blue, Green, Yellow, Orange, and Red, make wonderful transitions into one another – try them or have fun blending your own favorite tones and finishes. For this bracelet I used Frosted Violet (A), Metallic Dark Blue Iris (B), Opaque Turquoise Blue (C), Grass Green–lined Chartreuse (D), Frosted Canary Yellow (E), Frosted Ruby AB (F), and Orange AB (G).

WHAT YOU WILL NEED:

- 2g x size 11° seed beads in each of the 7 suggested colors (A, B, C, D, E, F, G)

- 12 x size 15° Czech Charlotte seed beads (H) (to anchor the daisy spacers)

- 6 x 5mm daisy spacers (J) (to complement the seed beads and clasp)

- 1 x 3-loop magnetic sliding clasp (or your chosen clasp)

1. With a good wingspan of thread and leaving a tail thread of 12" (30cm), cast on as many Hubbles in A as will comfortably span your wrist, bearing in mind that the clasp will add another ½" (1cm) to the overall length.

2. Work the 2nd row in B, not forgetting to ask that very important question for every stitch!

3. Work the 3rd row in C, the 4th in D and so on, until you have completed all 7 rows.

Attaching the clasp: I used magnetic sliding clasps for most of the linear Hubble projects in this book, as they are pretty and easy to attach, but feel free to use your own preferred clasp or closure method.

Use the working thread to attach this end of the strip to the loops on one side of the clasp via the arm beads, and the tail thread to do likewise at the opposite end of the strip for the other side of the clasp.

Designate numbers 1–7 for the rows (1 being the 7th row you worked, and #7 the foundation row). The 7-row width of the strip is just right to span the length of the clasp, however, only the arm beads at each end of rows 2, 4, and 6 will be the attachment points, as they roughly correspond with the three loops; the best fit is achieved thus:

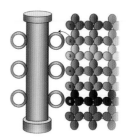

4   Pass around the final Hubble once more for security, and, following the established thread path, weave down and around to emerge from the top side of the unattached arm bead of row 2.

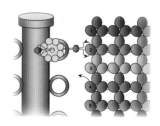

5   Pick up 1H and pass through the first loop of one side of the clasp. Pick up 1J, 1H and, missing out the H bead, pass back down through J, the loop and the first H bead picked up, and continue through the arm bead to emerge as before (see step 4 diagram).

Snuggle up and repeat this circuit for security, then weave on to emerge from the arm bead of row 4.

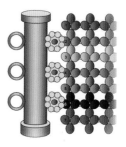

6   Connect the 2 remaining loops in the same way, and finish off.

7   Connect the other end of the strip to the corresponding clasp loops in the same way, using the tail thread, and finish off.

Variations

- Color and bead finish alone can radically change the finished effect.

- Try working the bracelet in another bead size, possibly adding more rows to vary the width of the strip. Although larger beads can be more chunky, they will still show off the lattice quality of the stitch very effectively.

- Simply choose a beautiful multi-loop clasp as a feature and tailor the number of rows to the clasp length.

- A lovely variation of the Spectrum bracelet is to work a graduation of color shades from dark to light. Select ten shades of your favorite color, from dark to light. Work the foundation row in the darkest shade, and work each subsequent row with lighter and lighter shades, as Jean did for her blues bracelet, page 16.

- As you have seen, working rows horizontally widens the strip, but try working rows vertically to lengthen it. Cast on, let's say ten Hubbles, and then stitch enough rows to span your wrist. Work it all in one color for a strong effect or try working a multicolored cuff. If you want to spread out the color changes evenly, work a test swatch to calculate how many rows you will need to encircle your wrist (don't forget to factor in the width of the clasp), then divide that number by however many colors you have chosen. To bead a vertical rainbow that spans your wrist, roughly divide the total number of rows required by seven to find out how many rows must be worked for each color. The clasp will be similarly attached to the head and body beads instead of the arm beads, and the finished effect is that the Hubbles appear to flow around your wrist.

- Don't just change color with a new row, try melting the colors into each other, by working one or two transition rows where two colors meet. The transition rows may consist of alternating stitches of the two blending colors. This would have a greater impact if worked in size 15° seed beads. The rainbow colors in Erika's bracelet (pages 6 and 23) have a one-row transition.

- Remember that each stitch is independent of its immediate neighbors within the row, so try creating random or symmetrical color patterns by working stitches in different colors.

- Try surface embellishing; randomly scatter pearls or crystals over the strip, by weaving them into the little spaces between Hubbles. Sandra added stripes of silver beads into her bracelet (page 35) and surface-embellished with pearls.

SPEX VORTEX

Graduating bead sizes within a row beautifully highlights the complete individuality of each Hubble stitch. The beaded vortex created whirls on and on, and is a spectacular (sorry!) way to really see Hubble in action. I worked this vortex in these wonderfully earthy tones: Frosted Metallic Khaki and Dark Khaki Iris.

WHAT YOU WILL NEED:

- 2g x size 15° Czech Charlotte seed beads (A)

- 4g x size 15° seed beads (B)

- 10g x size 11° seed beads (C)

- 33g x size 8° seed beads (D)

- 30g x size 6° seed beads (E)

- 2 x jump rings

- 1 pair eyeglasses holder findings

1 With a good wingspan of thread, work 4 Hubble foundation stitches thus: 1st stitch in A, 2nd in B, 3rd in C, and 4th in D; step up.

2 Work the 2nd row of 4 stitches in the order: D, C, B, and A. Already you can start to see how the vortex will curl.

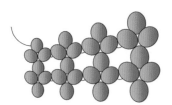

3 Repeat steps 1 and 2 until you are satisfied with the length of your vortex, finishing with an odd row (the example I worked is 325 rows long). Stitches for odd count rows will be in the order A to D, and for even count rows, D to A.

Step up to emerge from the head D bead.

4 Pick up 9B and pass through the D bead again, making a ring.

Pass around the ring once more for security, and on to emerge from the arm bead. Snuggle up.

This makes a little connecting loop to attach the glasses holder findings.

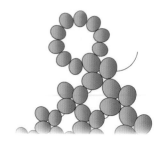

5 Pick up 1E and pass through the arm bead of the row below (effectively a peyote stitch even though the "turret" beads are slightly angled). Snuggle up.

6 Maintaining good, firm tension continue placing an E bead into each space between the arm beads of consecutive rows, along the entire length of the vortex. This creates a solid spine on the outer edge of the vortex, supporting its shape beautifully and causing it to really twirl around.

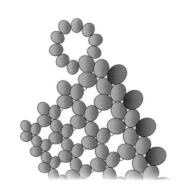

7 Weave around to emerge from the body D bead and work a connecting loop as before.

8 With the flat nose pliers, use the jump rings to attach the connecting loops to the eyeglasses holder findings.

Variations

- Don't stick to just one color; try blending, contrasting, and clashing colors and produce exciting, twirling stripes along the length of the beadwork.

- Experiment with different E beads for the spine, for example, triangles for a more serrated look.

LA NIÑA

With each new manipulation of the Hubble technique, I saw more and more possibilities – virtual exponential potential! It was plain as day that the logical evolution of the vortex was the wave. So the next step was to work a number of rows, watching the vortex curl approximately 120° in one direction, then just reverse the order of bead sizes and work the same number of rows to make it curl in the opposite direction – well, it would've been rude not to! For the La Niña bracelet I worked two wavy strips and entwined them together. I used the following colors: Marcasite/Steel (A), Gunmetal (B), Picasso Turquoise (C), Pale Blue–lined Crystal (D).

WHAT YOU WILL NEED:

- 1g x size 15° Czech Charlotte seed beads (A)

- 2g x size 15° seed beads (B)

- 5g x size 11° seed beads (C)

- 8g x size 8° seed beads (D)

- Clasp of choice (I used a silver-plated 2-loop magnetic sliding clasp)

1. With a good wingspan of thread, work 3 Hubble foundation stitches thus: 1st stitch in A, 2nd in B, and 3rd in C; step up.

2. The 2nd row will be in the reverse order (C, B and A).

3. Work a total of 11 rows.

4. 12th – 22nd rows (11 rows in total): Reverse the order of bead sizes, so the beadwork curls in the opposite direction. The smallest stitch will be worked over the largest, and conversely the largest worked over the smallest. The central bead size will not change, as the stitch count is odd, which guarantees a central stitch. As you can see, the Gunmetal beads appear to snake along the center, while the outer beads change and force the curves to change direction.

5 Continue reversing the bead size order every 11 rows, until you are satisfied with the length of your bracelet.

6 Finish off both the working and tail threads.

7 Leaving a tail thread of 10" (25cm), and starting at the foundation end, work in a new thread to emerge from the topside of the C arm bead.

8 Work a row of peyote stitches, placing a D bead into the spaces between arm beads along the length of the strip, weaving through to the opposite side every time the wave reverses.

9 Work an identical 2nd strip; arrange the 2 wavy strips so that the foundation end of one lies beside the head end of the other, then entwine the 2 strips together.

10 Position the final C Hubble of one strip over the foundation C Hubble of the other strip, mirroring it exactly, and stitch in place. Double-check the 2 strips are entwined evenly then secure the opposite ends in exactly the same way. Finally, attach the 2 most prominent end beads of each end to your chosen clasp.

Variations

· Try two contrasting strips entwined together. Erika used two colorways in her La Niña (image left). The wave colors correspond with each other and she has attached them at each junction, with the effect of chain links.

· Experiment with different bead sizes for gentler or stronger curves.

PROJECT 4

FANS

As you have now discovered, graduating bead size, stitch by stitch within a row, creates lovely rolling waves. However, try changing the bead size on a row-by-row basis and the result is gorgeous fan shapes. The Fans earrings project gives you a quick and easy taster of playing with horizontal bead size graduation, and you can have some embellishing fun with Czech Pip beads!

1 With A, cast on 6 Hubbles; work the 2nd row in B and the 3rd row in C.

With the working thread weave down to emerge from the body bead of the first foundation Hubble, carefully following the thread path. The thread will emerge from the inner side of the bead, that is, facing into the beadwork.

2 Finish off the tail thread.

Invert the beadwork so that the fan faces downwards, as it will when the earring is complete.

3 With the thread emerging from the A body bead on the left side of the fan, pick up 9A, 1D, 9A, and pass through the A body bead on the right side of the fan as in the diagram, creating an arch.

4 Pass back up the last 9A, emerging next to the D bead.

The arch attachment on the right side is now balanced on that A body bead, that is, there is thread emerging from both sides of the A body bead and passing up the 9A of the arch.

The left side of the arch attachment is not balanced because there is only one thread emerging from that A body bead and passing up the 9A.

5 You must balance it thus:

- Weave through D and down the 9A on the left side of the arch.
- Pass through the A body bead to emerge facing into the beadwork as before.
- Pass back up the 9A to emerge beside the D bead.

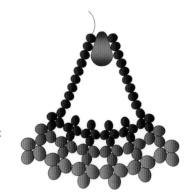

6 Pick up 7A and pass down the 9A on the right side of the D bead. Following the thread path as in the diagram, weave on to emerge from the inner side of the C head bead.

Now for the final embellishment...

7 Pick up *1A, 1D, 1A, and pass through the next C head bead*.
Repeat from *to* 4 more times, and finish off.

Make the partner earring and attach the ear wires.

Variations

· Substitute crystals, pearls, or
drops for the Preciosa Pip™
beads.

CHAPTER THREE

2-Drop and 3-Drop Hubble

2-Drop Hubble

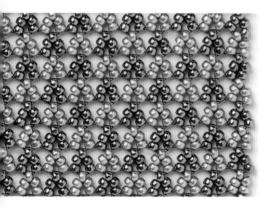

Now it's time to move on and see what else Hubble stitch has up its sleeve. When I first visualized 2-Drop Hubble, I was sitting on a train beading and my needle had just broken, so, unable to work it, I had to content myself with simply drawing the beads and thread path. I rushed home to give it a go and was absolutely delighted with the result. The beautiful repeating bead pattern was way beyond my expectations and I didn't stop that night until I'd made my first 2-Drop Hubble cuff.

Foundation Row:

Phase 1: Pick up 5 beads and make a ring by passing the needle again through the first 2 beads picked up, in the same direction.

For 2-Drop Hubble foundation stitches instead of picking up 3 beads for the body base, you are picking up 5.

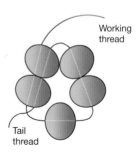

2 **Phase 2:** Pick up 1 bead and pass the needle through the adjacent 2 beads of the ring.

That completes one foundation 2-Drop Hubble stitch.

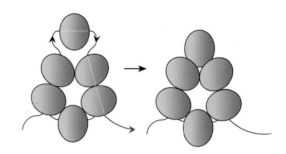

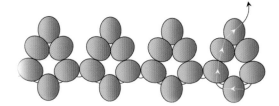

③ Snuggling up as you go to ensure each new stitch is gently touching the last, as in the diagram, repeat steps 1 and 2 a few more times. Weave around to emerge from the head bead to step up for the 2nd row.

Workshop Tip 4: *Here's the reality in the image above. As you experienced with basic Hubble, the individual stitches you have made won't all be standing upright, but again, you will deal with them when you work the 2nd row by* **asking the question.**

Workshop Tip 5: *As detailed in Workshop Tip 2 (page 20), when you look closely at your 2-Drop foundation row, you can clearly see a tiny gap between Hubbles that are facing in different directions. However, when I actually stitched them, they were just touching. There's no adjustment needed, because the gaps will disappear in the 2nd row when the upside-down stitches are swivelled upright again.*

The pretty 2-Drop pattern has now clearly manifested itself – I see the stitches as little firs or Christmas trees – and you will probably agree that it's a lot easier to determine whether a 2-Drop Hubble is the right way up or upside down.

2nd Row:

④ **1st Stitch – Phase 1:** Pick up 4 beads and make a ring by passing through the head bead below (from which the thread was emerging) in the same direction. Continue on through the first 2 beads just picked up.

As before with basic Hubble, this has effectively replicated the ring of beads that you made for each foundation stitch Phase 1, and now you are ready to place the head bead for Phase 2.

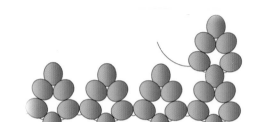

⑤ **Phase 2:** Pick up 1 bead and pass down through the 2 adjacent arm beads.

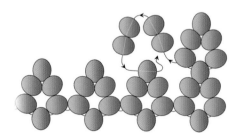

⑥ **2nd Stitch – Phase 1:** Pick up 4 beads, **ask the question**, and backstitch through the next adjacent head bead.

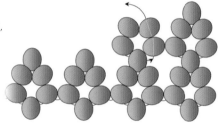

⑦ (Still in **Phase 1**): Continue on through the first 2 beads just picked up, in the same direction as before, making a ring, ready to place the new head bead.

Snuggle up!

8 **Phase 2:** Place the head bead as usual.

Complete the 2nd row working 2-Drop Hubbles as for the 2nd stitch, remembering to ask the question for each stitch. As usual there will be no need to ask the question during the 3rd row as all the 2-Drop Hubbles will be set upright.

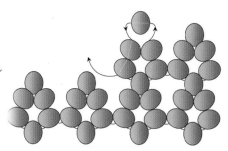

3-Drop Hubble

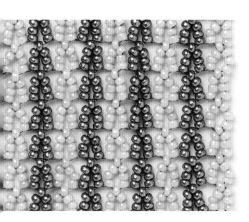

Progressing from 2-Drop to 3-Drop Hubble was an absolute must and followed on naturally in the development of Hubble stitch. Picking up 5 beads instead of 3 in Phase 1 produced the 2-Drop bead base; now you just need to add a further 2 beads in Phase 1 (7 beads in all), to produce the 3-Drop bead base.

To me, each 3-Drop stitch looks rather like a tall spruce tree, but it also makes a great daisy petal or flame.

Foundation Row:

1 **Phase 1:** Pick up 7 beads and make a ring by passing the needle again through the first 3 beads picked up, in the same direction.

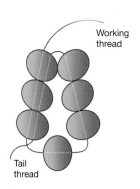

Working thread

Tail thread

Phase 2: Pick up 1 bead and pass the needle through the adjacent 3 beads of the ring.

That completes one foundation 3-Drop Hubble stitch.

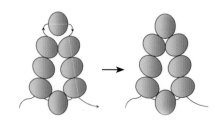

Snuggling up as you go, stitch some more 3-Drop Hubbles and step up as usual for the 2nd row.

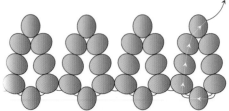

2nd Row:

1st Stitch – Phase 1: Pick up 6 beads and make a ring by passing through the head bead below (from which the thread was emerging) in the same direction. Continue on through the first 3 beads just picked up.

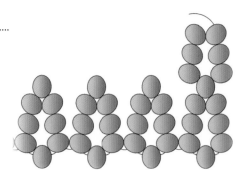

Phase 2: Pick up 1 bead and pass down through the 3 adjacent arm beads.

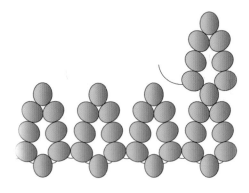

6 **2nd Stitch – Phase 1:** Pick up 6 beads, and backstitch through the next adjacent head bead.

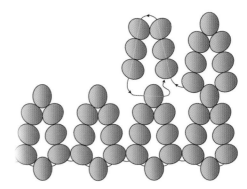

7 (Still in **Phase 1**): Continue on through the first 3 beads just picked up, in the same direction as before, making a ring, ready to place the new head bead.

Snuggle up!

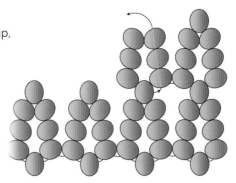

8 **Phase 2**: Place the head bead as normal.

Complete the 2nd row working the 3-Drop Hubbles as for the 2nd stitch (steps 6–8).

You'll have the opportunity to play with 3-Drop Hubble in Project 12 – Solar Flares (see Chapter 7).

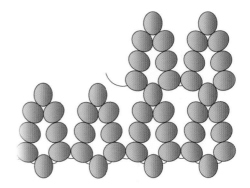

MERCURY

Practice and repetition is the best way to get to know a stitch, and making this elegant, slinky cuff in 2-Drop Hubble will help you do just that. Worked entirely in metallic silver, the Mercury cuff really shows off this beautiful textile to the max!

WHAT YOU WILL NEED:

- 18g x size 11° seed beads (A)

- Clasp of choice (I used a 7-loop sliding magnetic clasp, daisy spacers, and Czech Charlotte size 15° seed beads)

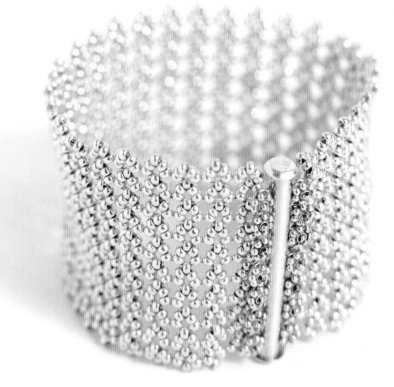

1. With a good wingspan of thread, cast on as many 2-Drop Hubbles in A as will comfortably span your wrist, bearing in mind that the clasp will add another ½" (1cm) to the overall length. Keep checking your tension is smooth and even, to guarantee a beautiful finish.

2. Work 10 rows in all.

3. Attach your chosen clasp. If using a 7-loop clasp, you will have to work out the best fit for the ends of the middle 8 rows, leaving the 1st and 10th row ends free.

Variations

· Embellish your 2-Drop Hubble with a little crystal between each of the head beads.

· Why not count the spaces between the head beads and see if you can place crystals or pearls between them in an organized pattern? For her version of this cuff, Gwenda changed color every other row, adding a single row of matching crystals for each color (page 4).

· The Mercury cuff is worked horizontally so it grows in width, but remember you can work a vertical strip that grows in length around your wrist.

CHAPTER FOUR

Horizontal Spaced Out
Hubble (HorSO)

Horizontal Spaced Out Hubble (HorSO)

One of the most exciting and unique features of the Hubble technique is the individuality of each stitch within a row. This means you could potentially work every single stitch in a different color. Now there's a thought! However, it also means that each stitch can be separated from its neighbors on either side by another bead or crystal, but still maintain its integrity – I call this Horizontal Spaced Out Hubble or HorSO for short. It's horizontal because the spacing out occurs within a row between stitches, and yes, you guessed it, there's also Vertical Spaced Out Hubble (VerSO), which is spacing out between rows! And of course, you can also space them out in both dimensions at the same time! But steady on, first things first! Get to grips with HorSO Hubbling and you will not only be able to make very pretty, linear textiles, but also have another useful technique to tailor your beadwork for beaded beads or bezelling cabochons.

It's helpful at first to practice HorSO in basic Hubble stitch and two contrasting colors, one for the Hubbles (A) and one for the spacer beads (B). The HorSO Hubble technique is simply to pick up a spacer bead before you pick up the usual Phase 1 beads for the body base, and then you ignore it! So let's have a go at HorSO Hubbling!

Foundation Row:

(1) With A, work one foundation Hubble.

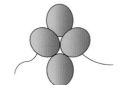

(2) **Phase 1:** Pick up 1B, 3A. Missing out the B bead, pass again through the first A bead picked up, forming a ring of the 3A only.

See what I mean about ignoring the spacer bead?

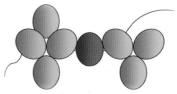

(3) Snuggle up so that they are all just touching.

If they are snuggled too tightly, the stitches can become unaligned and appear to be curving around. Again this just needs a little practice and will soon become automatic.

(4) Work **Phase 2** as for normal Hubble.

Snuggle up!

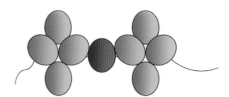

So that's 2 Hubbles separated by a spacer bead.

Repeat steps 2–4, working some more HorSOs and step up ready for the 2nd row.

Workshop Tip 6: *The image above shows a real row of HorSO. As before, I have purposely not carefully arranged the stitches, so you can see exactly what to expect. The stitches are absolutely fine and will behave when you work through the 2nd row, so there is no need to try and coerce them into perfection. The only thing that really matters is that they are snuggled up nicely and not too tightly.*

2nd Row:

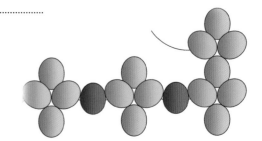

5   Work the 1st stitch of the 2nd row as normal (for a reminder see steps 7–8, page 22).

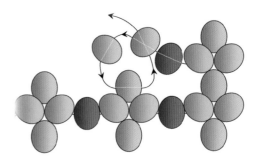

6   **Phase 1:** Pick up 1B, 2A. Missing out the B bead, **ask the question** and backstitch through the next head bead as usual.

Continue on through the first of the 2A beads just picked up, ready to place the head bead in Phase 2.

7 Snuggle up!

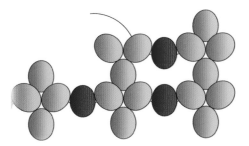

8 Work **Phase 2**, placing the head bead as normal.

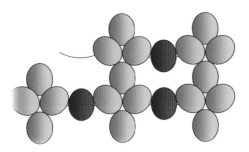

Repeat steps 6–8 to the end of the row and step up as normal.

Remember that after the 2nd row, you won't need to ask the question any more.

CRYSTAL LADDER

This is a great way to practice the HorSO technique with 2-Drop Hubble and large spacer beads. Not only does the bracelet work up really quickly, but also the large crystal spacers clearly define the attractive shape of the 2-Drop Hubbles. The flattened shape of these crystals allows them to overlap slightly; this creates lots of movement and sparkle. The seed beads I used had a lovely, frosted turquoise luster with a hint of lavender so I teamed them up with alternating indicolite and tanzanite crystals. You may find frosted beads a little resistant to snuggling, as they seem to grip the thread more, but they will shift with a bit of pressure.

WHAT YOU WILL NEED:

- 5g x size 11° seed beads (A)

- 20 x Swarovski mini rounds (1st color – B)

- 20 x Swarovski mini rounds (2nd color – C)

- 2 x 5-hole daisy links

- 8 x size 15° seed beads (to lock the links in place) (D)

- 2 x headpins

- Ball magnetic clasp (or your chosen clasp)

1. With a good wingspan of thread and using A, cast on 4 2-Drop Hubbles, placing a B spacer between the 2nd and 3rd stitches only.

2. Remembering to ask the question, work the same sequence of stitches for the 2nd row using a C spacer. Make sure there's plenty of snuggling up going on.

3. Continue working these alternate rows until the strip spans your wrist, making allowance for the width of the clasp. Step up to emerge from the end head bead.

4. Attach your chosen clasp via the head and body beads. I attached the clasp in this example thus:

   · Pass a headpin through the central hole of the 5-hole daisy link and the shank on one side of the magnetic clasp. Form a wrapped loop and cut off the excess wire. Repeat for the other side of the clasp.

   · Match the working end of the Hubble strip to the daisy link holes. The head and body beads correspond really well with the 4 remaining holes of each of the links.

   · Anchor each of the 4 head beads to the link with a C bead, then finish off.

   · Repeat for the body beads on the other end.

Variations

· Try different types and sizes of spacer bead, for example-rice pearls or size 15° seed beads

· Place spacers between every stitch!

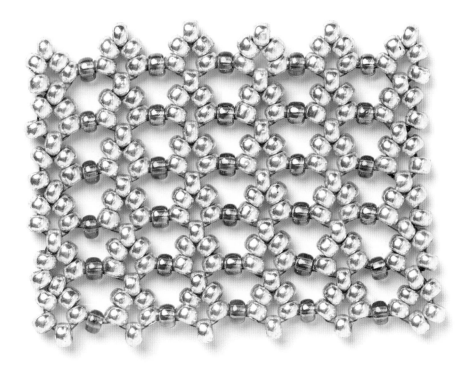

ENCHANTED FOREST

I had lots of fun with this project, not only because I was mixing Hubble stitches but also because I was playing with colors and used up many of my leftover beads. It was also interesting to note that a row of basic HorSO Hubble (where a size 11° seed bead is the spacer) was the same width as a row of 2-Drop Hubble, and that repeating these alternating rows created the effect of earth, tree trunks, and trees. I used Root Beer Brown for the HorSO (including the spacer beads) and a variety of colors for the 2-Drop trees.

WHAT YOU WILL NEED:

- 8g x size 11° seed beads (A)

- Variety of colors size 11° seed beads

- Clasp of choice (I used a 5-loop sliding magnetic clasp, daisy spacers, and Czech Charlotte size 15° seed beads as anchors)

1. With a good wingspan of thread and using A for both the Hubbles **and** the spacer beads, cast on 7 stitches in HorSO Hubble. Here's a quick refresher to get you started. Make one normal basic Hubble, but for the next stitch pick up 4A (the first A is the spacer, the last 3A are for the Phase 1 bead base). Ignore the spacer bead and make the bead base, then pick up 1A and put the head bead in place. Snuggle up. Continue until you have completed 7 stitches in all.

2. 2nd Row: Work the entire row in normal 2-Drop Hubble, using a different color for every stitch.

3. Repeat this alternating row sequence until you are satisfied with the length of the strip, ending with a HorSO Hubble row.

4. Attach your chosen clasp. If using a 5-loop clasp you will find the head/body beads of the central 5 stitches line up nicely with the loops.

Variations

· Thinking along the same lines, I imagined making a magical Narnia Forest version, using White Pearl Ceylon for the A beads as snow, and a brilliant peppering of transparent, AB, silver-lined crystal, and bright blues of all shades and finishes for the trees.

CHAPTER FIVE

Vertical Spaced Out
Hubble (VerSO)

Vertical Spaced Out Hubble (VerSO)

In the last chapter you saw how the HorSO technique widens Hubble beadwork, separating stitches within a row. Now we'll move on to Vertical Spaced Out Hubble or VerSO, which lengthens the Hubble textile by adding distance between rows – and this really can cause the beadwork to grow quickly.

The diagrams on the next page show how to work the VerSO technique in basic Hubble, but as VerSO is based on the addition of one or more beads on top of the head bead, that is, during Phase 2 of Hubble stitch, it can be used for basic, 2-Drop, and 3-Drop Hubble if desired.

To date I have worked with three different VerSO methods, each of which lengthens the beadwork by a differing amount, which is very helpful for bezelling or when you need to span a gap. Thus all three merit a place in your Hubbling arsenal, providing that exact spacing needed or delicious opportunities to embellish further. Of course, you could stitch normal Hubbles and then extend the distance between rows by working back along the row just completed, adding the spacer beads separately. However, it's important to get the three VerSO techniques under your belt because they minimize the number of passes you make through the beads; this allows you to Hubble with very small beads and create really beautiful, filigree beadwork especially when bezelling crystals.

VerSO-1 (Adding 1 spacer bead)

This VerSO technique can only be used for Hubble-in-the-round (see Chapter 6). Once you've had a go at either circular or tubular Hubble, the reason will become much clearer.

Foundation Row:

① Using one color, work **Phase 1** of a normal foundation Hubble (shown already completed in the diagram).

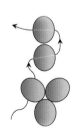

Phase 2: Pick up 2 beads (the 1st is the head bead, the 2nd is the spacer and will actually become a body bead in the next row).

The diagram shows the Phase 2 beads one above the other, exactly as they will be positioned shortly, when the slack thread is tightened.

② (Still in **Phase 2**): Pass again through the head bead (the first bead picked up) in the same direction.

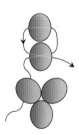

③ (Still in **Phase 2**): Continue through the arm bead as usual.

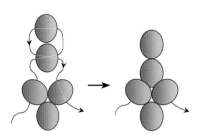

The first of these two diagrams shows the exact thread path achieved in completing the Phase 2 pass, before the stitch is snuggled up.

Workshop Tip 7: *Snuggle up by gripping the spacer and head beads between finger and thumb, as you pull the thread with the other hand to take up the slack.*

The spacer bead is nicely balanced on top of the head bead as if it's been ladder-stitched on; both their holes are parallel.

Continue casting on VerSO-1 Hubbles in this way.

Workshop Tip 8: *The image above shows a real row of VerSO-1. They will look higgledy-piggledy and will definitely not be behaving, but as always, the 2nd row will sort them out. As you work through the 2nd row you may find that some of the spacer beads are doubled over and aren't sitting perfectly on top of the head beads (the 4th, 5th, 6th and 7th Hubbles from the left in the image are doing exactly that); this doesn't affect the tension or the look of the beadwork, as stitching the 2nd row pulls them into position. It does mean that you need to make sure you pass the needle through the spacer bead and not accidentally through the head bead.*

Heads up! At the beginning of this section I stated that you can only use this method when working circular or tubular Hubble, and here's why:

4   As mentioned in Workshop Tip 3 (page 22), when you step up to work a new row of Hubble, the thread must emerge facing away from the beadwork.

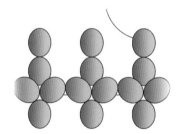

BUT... When you work a foundation row of VerSO-1 and step up for the next row, the thread will emerge in the wrong direction. So this step up is going nowhere!

Don't worry, there is a solution!

5   For circular or tubular Hubble, this is not a problem because when you join the first and last Hubbles together and then step up (as in the diagram), you can continue in the same direction for the new row.

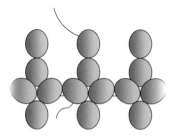

2nd Row:

6   Work the 2nd row, building the Phase 1 body beads as normal and remembering to pick up the spacer bead with each head bead in Phase 2.

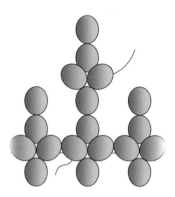

Don't forget to ask the question for every 2nd row stitch, although it will be a lot easier to see their orientation.

Practice VerSO-1 in Project 11 – Scarf Ring (see Chapter 6).

VerSO-2 (Adding 2 spacer beads – Albion or fringe style)

Although this method involves a few steps for each stitch, with practice you will gain a rhythm; the end result is entirely worth it, producing a pretty, open-weave lattice, so it merits a little perseverance.

Foundation Row:

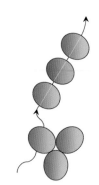

1. Use 2 colors (A for the main, B for the spacer). With A, work **Phase 1** of a normal foundation Hubble (shown already completed in the diagram).

   Phase 2: Pick up 1A, 1B, 1A.

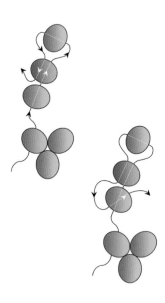

2. (Still in **Phase 2**): Missing out the last A picked up, pass through:

   · B in the opposite direction...

   · the first A picked up (head bead) in the same direction as before...

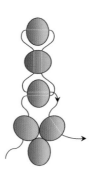

· and finally through the arm bead as usual, to complete the stitch.

This last diagram shows the exact thread path achieved in completing the Phase 2 pass, before it has been snuggled up.

This is like a tiny fringe or Albion stitch on top of the head bead; the B spacer bead lies perpendicular to both A beads, therefore so is its hole.

Workshop Tip 9: *Snuggle up by gripping the 2 spacer beads between finger and thumb, as you pull the thread firmly with the other hand to take up the slack.*

Workshop Tip 10: *As you can see in this real row of VerSO-2, the Phase 2 extensions don't all behave and sit perfectly on top of the head bead. It's no cause for concern because they can be coerced into position now while working the 2nd row. Fireline especially helps here, as it's nice and slip-slidey, making it easy for you to glide them into place.*

All of the stitches in the image above have been snuggled correctly, but as they swivelled independently, the tiny gap appeared – take a quick look back at Workshop Tip 2 (page 20) for the explanation.

3 Repeat steps 1 and 2 to cast on a few more VerSO-2 Hubbles.

Step up by following the normal thread pathway around the last Hubble, through the spacer above and the new body bead, to emerge as in the diagram.

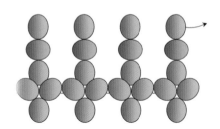

2nd Row:

4 Work the 2nd row, building the **Phase 1** body beads as normal and remembering to pick up the spacer beads with each head bead in **Phase 2**.

Play with VerSO-2 in Project 8 – Christmas Cuff (see this chapter).

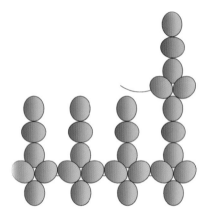

VerSO-3 (Adding 2 spacer beads – Ladder style)

This method also involves a few steps for each stitch, but practice brings perfection and a rhythm as with VerSO-2. The latticework structure formed by VerSO-3 is very strong and absolutely invaluable when bezelling cabochons; it's very similar to VerSO-2 but the extension is that tiny bit longer because the spacer beads are both parallel to the head bead. That extra smidgeon of distance can mean a lot when working out how to fit your beadwork around a cabochon. The other advantage of VerSO-3 for bezelling is that the spacer bead hole is superbly orientated for connections and further beading from it.

Foundation Row:

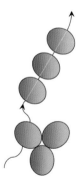

1. Use 2 colors (A for the main, B for the spacer). With A, work **Phase 1** of a normal foundation Hubble (shown already completed in the diagram).

   Phase 2: Pick up 1A, 1B, 1A.

   Heads up! This is the exact start as for VerSO-2, but now everything changes.

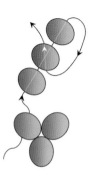

2. (Still in **Phase 2**): Missing out the last A picked up, pass through:

   · B in the same direction as before...

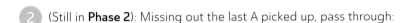

- the first A picked up (head bead) in the same direction as before...

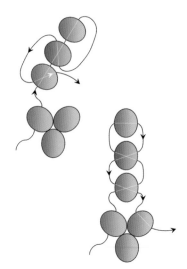

- and finally through the arm bead as usual, to complete the stitch.

This last diagram shows the exact thread path achieved in completing the Phase 2 pass, before it has been snuggled up.

Both spacer beads are nicely balanced on top of the head bead as if ladder-stitched; this time the B spacer bead is parallel to both A beads, therefore all their holes are parallel.

3 Work some more VerSO-3 Hubbles and step up, following the thread pathway, to emerge as in the diagram.

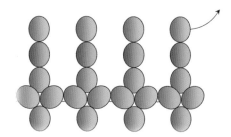

2nd Row:

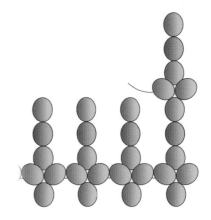

④ Work the 2nd row, building the Phase 1 body beads as normal and remembering to pick up the spacer beads with each head bead in Phase 2.

Rivolis cry out for some VerSO-3 Hubbling and Project 12 – Solar Flares does just that (See Chapter 7).

Workshop Tip 11: *Snuggle up by gripping the spacer beads between finger and thumb as you pull the thread with the other hand, really firmly to take up the slack – you can actually be a bit brutal as a good, tight tension is needed! Before you make the next stitch, grip the tail thread in one hand and the working thread in the other and tug to take up any remaining slack. If the stitches separate a little, snuggle up again. Do this for every stitch.*

Workshop Tip 12: *It's interesting to note that in a real foundation row of VerSO-3 because of all that brutal tension you have applied, when the Hubbles are in disorderly mode as above, they snuggle themselves up tightly. They actually look as if they're too tightly snuggled, not just touching. This is because there's a general force on the thread, pulling backwards into the ladder-stitched beads, so the gap threads you would normally see are disappearing a little, back into the ladder stitching. Don't be concerned – as always, when you correct them into their upright positions while stitching the 2nd row, the ladders will tighten up and all will be equal again!*

When using this technique for bezeling, especially over the edge of the cabochon, the extensions will generally correct themselves, as they would be under a fair degree of tension (the same applies to the VerSO-2 technique).

CHRISTMAS CUFF

With a little color play and stitch mixing, I put the definitive 2-Drop Hubble shape to good use. For the tiny Christmas scene a tree, topped with a silver star, stands in a red base, surrounded by a sprinkling of snow; this is worked in HorSO 2-Drop Hubble with VerSO-2 spacing the rows. The colors I used were: Dark Blue–lined Green AB (A), Silver-lined Ruby (B), Silver-lined Crystal (C), and White Pearl Ceylon (D).

WHAT YOU WILL NEED:

- 8g x size 11° seed beads (A)

- 1g x size 11° seed beads (B)

- 1g x size 11° seed beads (C)

- 1g x size 11° seed beads (D)

- Clasp of choice (I used a 5-loop sliding magnetic clasp and daisy spacers with the D beads as anchors)

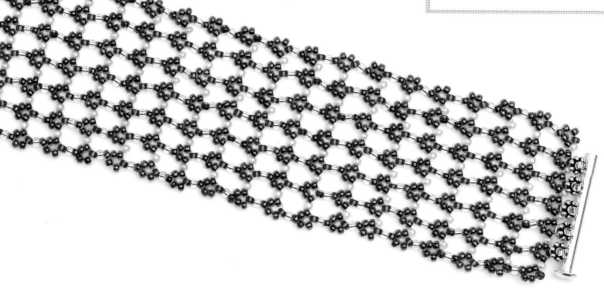

Foundation Row:

1ST STITCH:

1 **Phase 1:** Pick up 4A, 1B, and pass through the first 2A picked up.

2 **Phase 2:** Pick up 1A, 1C, 1B, and work Phase 2 as for VerSO-2.

2ND STITCH:

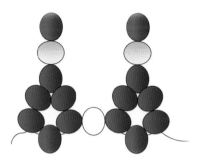

3 **Phase 1:** Pick up 1D, 4A, 1B and pass through the first 2A picked up.

4 **Phase 2:** Repeat Phase 2 as for the first foundation stitch.

Repeat the 2nd foundation stitch 5 more times (7 stitches wide in total).

Work as many rows as you need to span your wrist, BUT the final row will not need any VerSO, so just work the normal Phase 2 for each stitch.

Attach your chosen clasp or, if using the 5-loop clasp, the central 5 head beads or body beads at each end of the strip will correspond with the loops on each side of the clasp and can be anchored in place with daisy spacers and the silver D beads.

CHAPTER SIX

*Hubble-in-the-Round
(Circular and Tubular Hubble)*

Hubble-in-the-Round (Circular and Tubular Hubble)

Writing this book has been a fascinating journey and, along the way, it has also helped me consolidate my thoughts about my beadwork. For me, one of the most exciting aspects of beading is the challenge of bezelling objects such as crystals and cabochons; I am absolutely passionate about trapping them in delicate beaded structures, especially using the very tiny size 15° Charlotte seed beads. It suddenly became apparent to me that for the last several years I had been on a kind of mission to trap crystals in as little beadwork as possible, modifying the techniques I used to strip away as many beads as I could, while still maintaining a strong structure. Hubble-in-the-round (Hubble stitch in its circular or tubular forms) is superb for bezelling, as its lacy quality allows more of the crystal sparkle or pearly gleam to show. The stitches appear to take on an almost eery quality of floating against the cabochon surface. This is particularly prominent when using the tinier seed beads.

To work in circular or tubular Hubble, once you have cast on a row of any of the Hubble stitches, you just need to join the working end to the tail end.

1. Cast on the required number of Hubbles for your circular or tubular piece and bring the tail and working ends of the beadwork together.

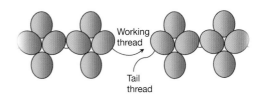

2. Pass up into the arm and on through the head bead. Look closely at this connection – the 2 end Hubbles are joined under their arms, just like all the others.

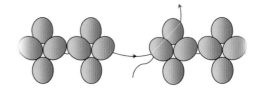

3. Snuggle up the 2 ends of the beadwork.

How easy was that?

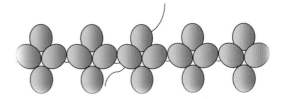

Workshop Tip 13: *Don't worry about trying to orientate everything correctly. This may look a little messy, but the great news is you don't need to fiddle around trying to get the Hubbles to stand upright. As you work the 2nd row and ask the question, they will all be orientated correctly.*

Workshop Tip 14: *For strength and security to prevent the two ends moving apart, weave on to emerge from the head bead of the next Hubble along and snuggle up to be sure. When finishing off the tail thread, you may need to work around the first Hubble, so this eliminates the problem of too many thread passes.*

For extra security, particularly when bezelling, pass around all 4 beads of this 2nd Hubble, to emerge once more from the head bead.

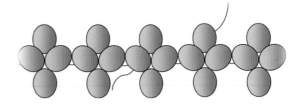

SNOWFLAKES

Here's a lovely little project to get you using the join for circular Hubble and playing with basic and 2-Drop HorSO Hubble; it's even got a super, easy-peasy way of casting on. I used Frosted Chalk White (A) and White Alabaster (B) beads for the Snowflakes.

WHAT YOU WILL NEED:

- 0.5g x size 15° seed beads (A)

- 12 x size 11° seed beads (B – spacer beads)

- 2 x 3mm jump rings

- 1 pair ear wires

1 Pick up 6A and pass through all 6A again to form a ring. Pass through the first A picked up again.

Think of each of these 6 beads as a head bead from a Hubble row below. Now you can build a row of Hubbles from them thus:

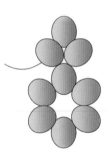

2 Pick up 2A and work a Phase 1 bead base onto the bead from which the thread was emerging. Then add the head bead for Phase 2.

3 Now you've completed 1 Hubble, build 5 more, snuggling up along the way.

Join the 6th to the 1st to complete the circle.

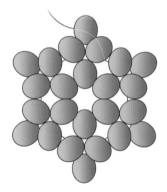

Workshop Tip 15: *Secure the circle either by passing on to the next Hubble head bead, or pass around all 4 beads of the first Hubble, emerging from the head bead.*

As always, snuggle up.

4 With A, work a 2-Drop Hubble.

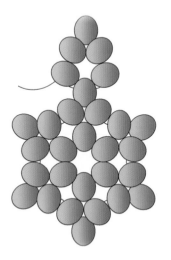

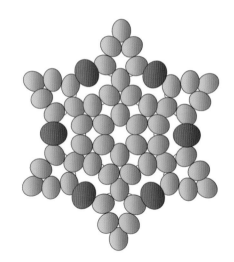

⑤ Work 5 stitches of HorSO 2-Drop Hubble, using B as the spacer bead.

Pick up the final B spacer bead before joining the 6th stitch to the 1st to complete the circle.

Finish off both the working and tail threads.

⑥ To complete the earring, attach a jump ring and ear wire.

> **Workshop Tip 16:** *Remember, two stitches are always joined by a thread coming from under their touching arms, so for circular or tubular 2-Drop Hubble you will be passing the needle up through the 2 beads of the arm, continuing on to emerge from the head bead.*

Variations

· Using contrasting colors for the two rows produces really pretty results.

· Make a bracelet or necklace from lots of snowflakes in a multitude of colors, joined together. Erika worked a bracelet of snowflakes, using Czech SuperDuo® for some head beads to join the individual units (see image page 74).

· Try experimenting with more rows to see how you can extend Hubble-in-the-round, maintaining a flat piece or turning it tubular. Change Hubble and spacer bead sizes for, what I call, an organized freeform approach, and see what interesting shapes are produced. Or even work around a solid shape!

HUBBLE ROPES

These pretty ropes provide the perfect opportunity to practice tubular Hubble. With only four stitches per row you can whip 'em up in no time. As with lots of beadwork the fiddliest bit is at the start, but once you've worked the second row and settled the little foundation Hubbles, it really flows. The technique for the two rope examples shown here is exactly the same; the only difference is in where I chose to change bead color. Look at how lacy and spacey they are.

FOR A ROPE OF ONE COLOR, YOU WILL NEED:

- 8g x size 11° seed beads

- Clasp of choice (I used a 5mm wide magnetic clasp, attached with gimp to protect the connecting thread)

- 1 x cocktail stick

1 Cast on 4 Hubbles, join them into a circle, secure, and step up.

Workshop Tip 17: *Here's where the cocktail stick comes in. It's really helpful to pass the stick through the center of the ring of 4 Hubbles. With the stick in place you can turn the foundation Hubbles to make sure they are all shouting "Hooray" and easily see where you're going to pass the needle for each stitch. Keep the stick in your beadwork for several rows or until you can hold it easily. Be vigilant to ensure the thread doesn't get caught around the stick and form a loop.*

2 Continue working rows until you are satisfied with the length of the rope.

3 To finish off each rope end, run the needle around each of the 4 head or body beads a few times, drawing them together tightly. Attach a clasp component to each end and finish off.

To try the two rope variations shown below:

Rope 1 (Matte Metallic Purple (A) and Pale Green-lined Crystal (B))

WHAT YOU WILL NEED:

- 4g x size 11° seed beads (A)
- 4g x size 11° seed beads (B)

1 Foundation Row: Cast on 4 stitches alternating the colors (A, B, A, B). Join the 2 ends to form a circle, secure, and step up, emerging from an A bead.

2 2nd Row: Work stitches in the order B, A, B, A.

3 Continue repeating this 2-row pattern sequence until you achieve the required length.

Rope 2 (Ceylon Pale Tangerine (A), Duracoat Galvanized Berry (B), Dark Topaz Rainbow Gold Luster (C) and Frosted Matte Bronze Iris (D))

WHAT YOU WILL NEED:

- 2g x size 11° seed beads (A)
- 2g x size 11° seed beads (B)
- 2g x size 11° seed beads (C)
- 2g x size 11° seed beads (D)

1. Foundation Row: Cast on 4 stitches, each one a different color (A, B, C, D). Join the 2 ends to form a circle, secure, and step up, emerging from an A bead.

2. 2nd Row: Work stitches in the order A, B, C, D.

3. Continue repeating the sequence until you achieve the required length.

Variations

- There are so many variation possibilities for this technique. You saw what happens if you use a different color for every stitch in Project 7 – The Enchanted Forest (see Chapter 4); now that would be a fun rope to make! What about all different shades of blue or purple? Or...

- A 2-Drop Hubble rope is so much more open and lacy; it would also grow very quickly!

SCARF RING

Here's a lovely little design to give you plenty of practice in combining HorSO and VerSO-1 Hubble in tubular form. Phew! That might sound challenging but it's not when you take it one step at a time. You'll be working the stitches automatically before long. There's also the opportunity to have fun embellishing with crystals and a fringe at the end. The structure gains rigidity with the crystals in place, making it perfect for its role. Choosing beads to complement the scarf, I used Ceylon Sky Blue (A) and Transparent Turquoise AB (B), with Metallic Blue crystals (C).

WHAT YOU WILL NEED:

- 5g x size 11° seed beads (A)
- 1g x size 11° seed beads (B – spacer beads)
- 78 x 4mm Swarovski® bicone crystals (C)

Workshop Tip 18: *Look closely at the image; the foundation row is at the top and the fringe is worked from the final row.*

Foundation Row:

1 **1st stitch**: With a good wingspan, pick up 3A and work Phase 1.

Pick up 2A and work **Phase 2** as for VerSO-1.

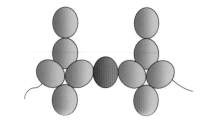

2 **2nd stitch**: Pick up 1B, 3A, and work Phase 1 (remember the 1B is the spacer).

Pick up 2A and work **Phase 2** as for VerSO-1.

Snuggle up – refer to Workshop Tip 7 (page 60).

3 Repeat step 2 eleven times, making a total of 13 stitches.

Before you join the 2 ends pick up 1B for the final spacer.
Secure and step up.

2nd Row:

4. Work a row of HorSO only, with no VerSO-1 (so only pick up 1A for every Phase 2). Step up.

5. These 2 rows form the pattern to be repeated, so to continue, the 3rd row will be HorSO combined with VerSO-1, and the 4th Row will be HorSO only.

   Continue until you have worked 8 rows in all.

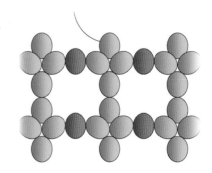

6. Secure the final join and weave around to emerge from the nearest body bead, ready to begin embellishing with the crystals.

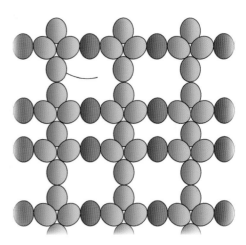

7 Pick up 1C and pass through the next body bead of the same row.

Repeat 12 times to fill all the spaces in this row.

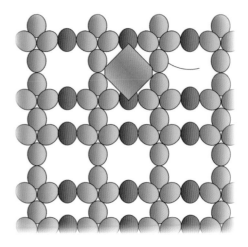

8 Look closely at the crystals; their holes should be centerd between head and body beads of adjacent Hubble rows. However there is only thread passing through the body beads and crystals. We're going to sort that out now.

Make sure you snuggle up, but not too tightly.

With the thread emerging from the same body bead as at the beginning of this row, turn and pass the needle through the head bead directly below, which reverses your direction.

Work around the row of crystals, passing instead through the head beads of the row below this time, and snuggle up. This balances the crystals correctly in their spaces.

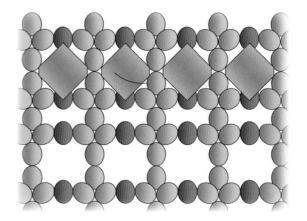

9 Fill all the remaining spaces with crystals, then weave back up to emerge from a head bead on the final row. Working from each head and spacer bead, build a fringe to your liking. It can be simple like the one in my example, or long and luscious, or frilly and loopy, or...!

Variations

- Work a scarf ring in 2-Drop Hubble and substitute pearls or different sized and shaped beads for the crystals.

- Make a real statement; work a 6-row version without the fringe for a fabulous ring!

CHAPTER SEVEN

Inverted Hubble

Inverted Hubble

What is inverted Hubble and where does it fit into the scheme of things? The answer is that it's simply Hubble stitches that are upside down, worked from existing Hubble stitches (or other available, presenting beads, but that's for another dimension or Book 2). So it's important to understand that a row of inverted Hubble will always be a new row worked from existing beadwork – it won't ever be a foundation row, because it has to be worked from something that's already there.

It's a very special part of Hubbling because it will get you bezelling crystals and cabochons in utterly delightful ways.

For this book, I am introducing you to inverted Hubble worked from circular Hubble because this demonstrates the technique very clearly and you can practice with the Solar Flares project. In Book 2 you will see ways of manipulating inverted Hubble to produce some stunning textiles.

Now back to business. By now you will have done a good bit of Hubbling, so you know that Hubble stitch always begins with Phase 1, the bead base, followed by Phase 2, the head bead. Fortunately, that also applies to inverted Hubble (hurray!); the only difference is that for Phase 1 you must always cast on a completely new, separate bead base (just like working a foundation Hubble) instead of incorporating the existing bead in the row below, and for Phase 2, instead of picking up a new head bead, you simply pass through the bead that is already presenting in the row below.

You might think right now it's time to reach for the bottle, but we're nearly there so stick with it, because this technique opens up so many interesting possibilities.

I suggest working with two bright colors of size 8° seed beads (A and B), to get a good look at the thread path and really understand what's going on. To set yourself up for a row of inverted Hubble you're going to work a small circle of basic Hubble.

Let's get started!

Foundation Row:

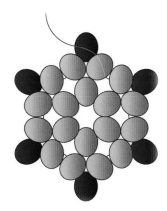

1. Using A beads for the Phase 1 body base and B beads for the Phase 2 head, work steps 1–3 as for Project 9: Snowflakes (see Chapter 6).

   Using the easy-peasy circular start ensures all the head beads are orientated correctly (so you don't have to worry about asking the question!), plus you can clearly see them as they are a different color!

Workshop Tip 19: *Remember how the 1st stitch of any 2nd row of Hubbling is a bit different from the rest because you are always working from the stitch directly below? Well, this is also true for inverted Hubble.*

2nd Row:

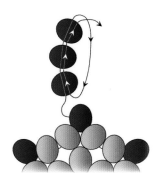

2. 1st inverted Hubble stitch, **Phase 1**: Pick up 3A and pass the needle through all 3A again to make a ring. This will dangle close beside the head bead from which the thread was emerging.

(Still in **Phase 1**): Snuggle up those 3A beads to complete the body base.

Don't worry that it's still not completely snuggled up to the rest of the beadwork yet.

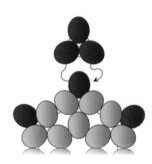

(3) **Phase 2**: Look closely at the head bead below, from which the thread was emerging. In the diagram the thread is emerging from the left side of the bead so pass the needle through from right to left. This correctly balances the body base on the head bead.

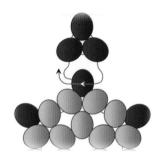

(4) (Still in **Phase 2**): To complete Phase 2 simply pass through the adjacent arm bead as usual and snuggle up.

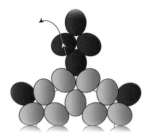

⑤ 2nd inverted Hubble stitch, **Phase 1**: Pick up 3A and pass once more through the first A picked up in the same direction (making the ring).

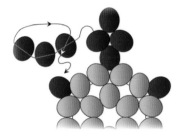

⑥ **Phase 2**: Snuggle the 3A together and pass forward (yes forward, do not backstitch) through the next presenting head bead.

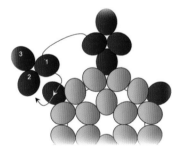

Heads up! The beads in the diagram are numbered 1, 2, and 3, which is the order in which they were picked up. Keep in mind that the thread is emerging from bead 1.

7 (Still in **Phase 2**): Pass through the adjacent arm bead (2).

Heads up! It's very easy at this point to accidentally pass through bead 3, which would cause the Hubble to twist, so take care not to.

The diagram is showing that no snuggling has happened yet, but that's so you can clearly see the thread path. Any second now...

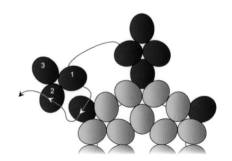

8 Snuggle up... and this is what happens when working in circular mode!

The 2 new inverted hubbles are pulled together and flip over the front of the beadwork, hinged via the head beads.

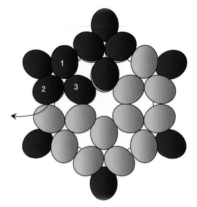

9 Repeat steps 5–8 four more times and join the 6th Hubble to the 1st
as for circular Hubble (remember the thread is emerging from under
the Hubble's arm, and the needle must pass up into the neighboring
arm from underneath and on through the head bead – see diagram).
Secure the join by passing around the 1st inverted Hubble once more.

Workshop Tip 22: *Notice how this sample has almost become a little parcel – something pretty could be slipped
inside and trapped in there by weaving around the 6 central beads, to mirror the first side. Try working this sample
in size 11° seed beads. It will allow you to practice inverted Hubble on a smaller scale, and you could trap a 6mm
rivoli or chaton in there! It makes a lovely little element.*

SOLAR FLARES

So here we are with the last project in the book, and I've thrown in just about everything including the kitchen sink! You will be working basic VerSO-3, inverted, 2-Drop and 3-Drop, Hubble, all in-the-round! This is also the perfect opportunity to play with gorgeous crystals and blend or contrast lots of bead colors. These lovely little Solar Flares can be used individually as pendants, connected together to make bracelets or necklaces, or even as decorative embellishments for simple beaded cuffs.

WHAT YOU WILL NEED FOR ONE SOLAR FLARE:

- 1g x size 15° seed beads (A)

- 1g x size 15° seed beads (B)

- 1 x 14mm Swarovski® rivoli

For the Solar Flare in the image I used Jet Black (A) and Duracoat Silver (B) with a Light Siam rivoli.

Heads up! Don't forget that because you will be using VerSO-3, the spacer beads will all be parallel to the head bead for each stitch.

1   Work the reverse side of the Solar Flare first. With 40" (1m) thread and using A for the body beads and the head bead, and B for both the spacers, work a row of 13 basic VerSO-3 Hubble stitches. Make sure there's lots of brutal snuggling to achieve a nice tight fit on the rivoli (refer to Workshop Tip 11, page 67)!

2   Join the 13th stitch onto the 1st, snuggle up, and pass around the 1st Hubble again for security. Weave on to emerge from the outermost spacer bead as in the diagram.

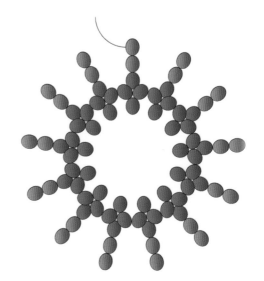

3   Now, using B, you are going to work a row of inverted Hubble from these outermost spacer beads.

As you snuggle up the 2nd stitch, the row will immediately curl over and begin to form the rivoli trap.

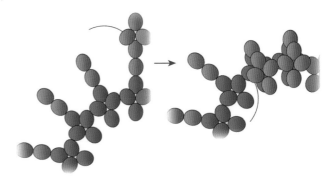

4 Work 8 more inverted Hubbles and slip the rivoli into the little pocket you've created.

The middle spacer beads of each stitch will perch precisely on the edge of the rivoli, but they may occasionally need a little gentle coercion not to twist and show their holes – use an awl or thick sewing needle to turn them into position gently, so their holes are parallel with the edge of the rivoli.

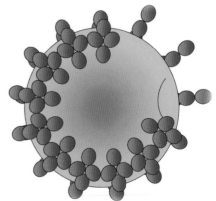

5 Work the last 3 stitches and make the final join. For security, run around the first stitch of the row and weave on to emerge from the central spacer bead sitting on the edge of the rivoli. Snuggle up!

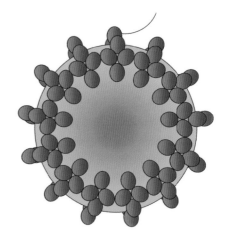

6 Using A, work a 3-Drop Hubble from the spacer bead.

Work 12 more stitches around the perimeter and make the join.
Weave around to emerge from the spacer bead once more.

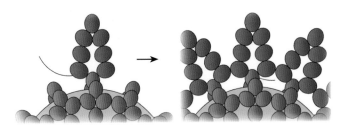

7 Using B, work a new row of 2-Drop Hubble in front of the 3-Drop row.

Finish off both the working and tail threads.

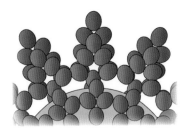

To make the bracelet, gather a collection of Solar Flares and connect them together via the 3-Drop stitches. Connecting them poses a slight challenge as there is no symmetry due to the odd number of stitches around each rivoli, but it can be overcome. As you can see in the image, for each connection, I slid the tip of one 3-Drop stitch between two 3-Drops on the next Solar Flare and ran the needle through the adjacent beads of the three touching stitches. Not wanting anything to detract from the pretty components, I chose an unobtrusive, little magnetic clasp, which is attached with gimp to protect the thread from its shank.

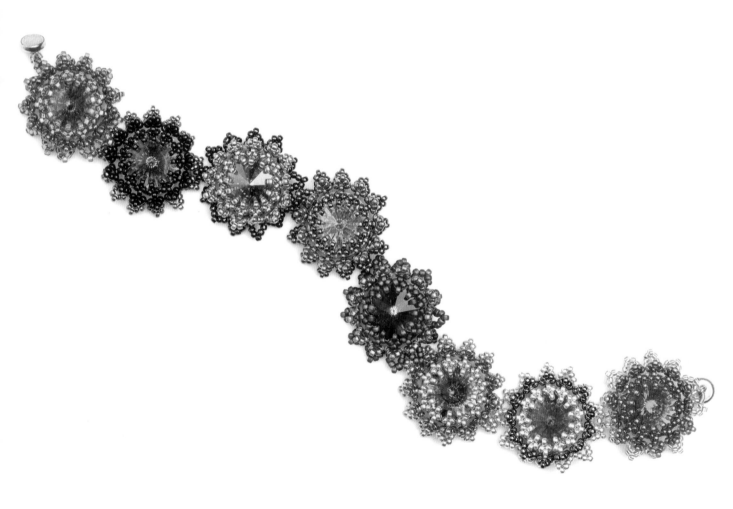

Variations

- Interchange A and B for the 3-Drop and 2-Drop rows; work only one or the other or neither and just connect the Hubbled rivolis!

- Make an entire necklace of Solar Flares – you'll need to connect them in a curve instead of a straight line.

The next part of the Hubbling journey...

You've come such a long way with me on this first exploration into Hubble stitch and now you have all the basic techniques at your fingertips. As you have seen, there are not only delightful varieties of Hubble stitch to bead, but also there is infinite scope for playing with colors and finishes to produce wonderfully different textiles, varying the bead sizes to make coils, curls, and twizzles and manipulating the stitches themselves to lengthen your beadwork, expand it, turn it into three-dimensional tubes and even crystal traps! The possibilities are breathtaking; if only there were 48 hours in every day!

I hope you've had lots of fun experimenting with Hubble, but we've only just begun! Join me in Book 2 to journey even deeper into planet Hubble, and explore the huge potential of this gorgeous new stitch!

THANKS AND ACKNOWLEDGEMENTS

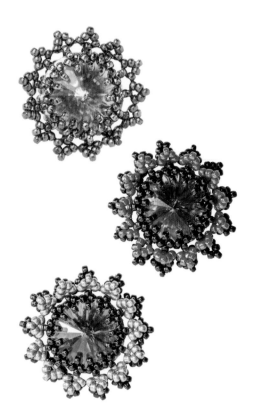

THANKS AND ACKNOWLEDGEMENTS TO...

Being the world's greatest procrastinator, I am still in a state of disbelief as to how *Hubble Stitch* has finally come to fruition. Usually when it comes to writing up my instructions, my house is spotless, the washing done, and the cat has been ironed; I do everything but sit down and write, it's even one of my best times to design. Although I had plenty of encouragement over the years from students, friends, and family, I couldn't imagine ever writing a book. When I made that first Hubble and then worked a second one next to it, I can only liken the feeling to being in a dark room and suddenly someone throwing on the light switch! I literally gasped. So, once I'd feverishly explored some of the ways to manipulate the stitch I knew I just had to write this book.

It's almost two years since that light illuminated my thoughts and, while I've thoroughly enjoyed the journey, it's been a steep learning curve in many ways. I had to believe in myself enough to do it and I want to thank my longtime, beady friend Sue Richardson for fostering and nurturing that belief. In fact, for years she's been encouraging me to write a book of my designs and finally it just felt right. I have nothing but praise for Sue and her wonderful publishing team, Kelly Mundt and Mark Hobin, who made the whole process smooth and painless due to their skill and professionalism.

Thanks must also go to another dear friend Heather Kingsley-Heath who was always there with soothing words and sage advice for the times when I felt writing and running my life was like climbing an endless mountain.

Special thanks go to Nitty Chamcheon, Gwenda Fairbairn, Sandra Fox, Erika Simons, and Jean Phillips, my lovely, beady friends from the Dangerous Beaders, without whose help and patience there would have been a lot of blank pages! They totally embraced Hubble stitch and then launched themselves with vim and vigor into beading some fabulous versions and variations of these projects.

The photography was going to be a very important issue for me, as I wanted everyone to really be able to see the structure of Hubble stitch, its beauty, and its fabulous potential, and for that I thank Michael Wicks.

Last but by no means least, for the times when beadwork and writing is top of my agenda, to know I have my family's constant love and support means everything to me.

Have fun Hubbling!

CONTACT DETAILS

Email: beadschool@gmail.com

Website: www.beadschool.co.uk

Facebook: Melanie de Miguel (Beadschool Mel)

YouTube: Beadschool – Melanie de Miguel

Twitter: @BeadschoolMel